Football File

DEFENDING and GOALKEEPING

James Nixon

Photography by Bobby Humphrey

W
FRANKLIN WATTS
LONDON • SYDNEY

This edition 2014

Franklin Watts
338 Euston Road
London NW1 3BH

Franklin Watts Australia
Level 17/207 Kent Street
Sydney NSW 2000

© Franklin Watts 2010, 2014

ISBN 978 1 4451 3105 4
Dewey classification number: 796.3'342

A CIP catalogue record for this publication
is available from the British Library.

Planning and production by
Discovery Books Limited
Editor: James Nixon
Design: Blink Media
Illustrations: Stefan Chabluk

The author, packager and publisher
would like to thank the children of
Farsley Celtic Junior Football Club for
their participation in this book.

Printed in China

Franklin Watts is a division
of Hachette Children's Books,
an Hachette UK Company.
www.hachette.co.uk

Photo acknowledgements:
Getty Images: pp. 5 bottom (Hamish Blair),
11 bottom (Andrew Yates/AFP), 15 (Malcolm
Couzens), 21 top (Javier Soriano/AFP), 25 bottom
(Patrick Stollarz/AFP), 29 centre-right (Tony
Quinn);   Shutterstock: pp. 2 (Andrey Yurlov), 4
(Jonathan Larsen), 5 top (Herbert Kratky), 6 (Titus
Manea), 7 middle-right (Sportsphotographer.eu),
9 bottom (Maxisport), 13 top (Mark Bolton), 14
(Jonathan Larsen),   17 bottom (Jonathan Larsen),
18 top (Andrey Yurlov), 19 top-left (Jonathan
Larsen), 22 (Jonathan Larsen), 23 right (Brandon
Parry), 24 bottom (Andrey Yurlov), 26 top
(Sportgraphic), 27 middle-right (Sportgraphic),
28 top (Matt Trommer), 28 bottom (Jonathan
Larsen), 29tl (Laszio Szirtesi), 29 bl (Maxisport).

Cover photos: Shutterstock: left (Sportgraphic),
right (Jonathan Larsen).

Every attempt has been made to clear copyright.
Should there be any inadvertent omission please
apply to the publisher for rectification.

Statistics on pages 28–29 are correct at the time
of going to press, but in the fast-moving world
of football are subject to change.

Contents

Words that appear in **bold** are in the glossary on page 30.

STOPPING goals

Defending is all about stopping the opposition scoring a goal. It may not seem as much fun, but keeping goals out is just as important as scoring them. All the best teams have a strong defence. Defence plays a big part in winning matches.

Put the pressure on

When your team loses the ball it's time to defend. It is not just defenders that are responsible for defending. The whole team, including midfielders and attackers, need to put pressure on the opposition when they are on the ball. When defending, you have two main aims. The most important thing is to try to put a stop to your opponent's attack. You must also try to regain **possession** of the ball for your team.

Opponents on the ball need to be pressurised in all areas of the pitch. This makes it harder for them to build an attack.

The back line

The last line of a team's defence are the defenders and goalkeeper. They must be determined and brave, and do all they can to stop the ball going into the net. Defenders spend their time marking attackers, tackling and clearing the ball to safety. Goalkeepers need to command their penalty area, catch crosses and make saves. More hinges on the goalkeeper than any other player. If the keeper makes a mistake the result can be disastrous.

EXPERT: Vincent Kompany

Belgian captain and defender Vincent Kompany (above, right) has all the **attributes** it takes to be a top defender. He is tall, strong, and dominant in the air and the tackle. Kompany is also willing to put his body on the line. In 2013, in a World Cup qualifying match, he played for 60 minutes with a broken nose and cracked eye socket after crashing into the opposition's goalkeeper.

EXPERT: Tim Howard

Tim Howard is the USA's number one goalkeeper and one of the top shot stoppers in the game. Like all good goalkeepers Howard also takes charge of his defence. Howard is constantly shouting at the defenders in front of him, to alert them to attackers and to get them into position (left).

CLOSING down

Closing down opponents and blocking them, known as jockeying, are two of the most vital parts of defending.

If you give attackers time and space, they will cut through your defence in a flash.

Jockeying

Jockeying slows down an opponent's attack and gives time for your defence to get into position. The pressure it puts on the attacker might force them into a mistake. Or you may be able to put in a tackle from the jockeying position.

The defensive stance

The defensive stance is the position your body should be in when jockeying. It is almost like being ready to pounce. Crouch low with your knees bent and your eyes on the ball. Stand on the balls of your feet and keep your arms out for balance. You should stay about one metre away from the attacker. Get too close and the attacker will dart past you. Too far away and you're not putting the player under enough pressure.

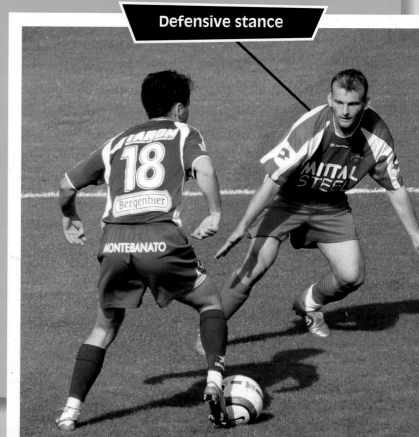

Defensive stance

6

Tips

▶ Close players down quickly, but slow down as you approach (1). If you rush in, off balance, the attacker can sidestep past you.

▶ Be patient. Stay on your feet and don't tackle unless you are sure you will win the ball. The most important thing is to stop the opponent moving forward. If you lunge in, the attacker can dodge around you.

▶ If you are jockeying on the move, force the attacker where you want them to go. You may want to guide the player out wide away from goal and danger (2). Or you can cover one side and force a player on to their weaker foot.

▶ If you are jockeying an opponent from behind, get tight to the player. Don't let them turn to face goal (3).

Shoulder barge

A shoulder barge is a useful way of getting the ball from your opponent. This is a form of body contact, but it is not a foul if done properly. Keep your arm close to your body, and using the top half of your arm lean in to the opponent and barge them away from the ball. Don't raise your arm. This is pushing and a foul.

TACKLING

A tackle is one of the best ways to get the ball off your opponent. To tackle well, you must be determined, have good technique and excellent timing. Here are some of the techniques you need to learn.

Keep it clean

Make sure you tackle the ball first and not the player. To give away a foul is bad for your team. Never raise your studs, tackle a player from behind or tackle with two feet. These tackles are dangerous and could seriously injure your opponent.

Block tackle

Use a block tackle when you are face to face with an opponent. When making this tackle you can stay on your feet and move off with possession of the ball.

- ▶ Plant your non-tackling foot on the ground to give you a firm base.
- ▶ Lean forward to get your whole weight behind the tackle (1).
- ▶ With your eye closely on the ball, tackle with the inside of your foot (2).
- ▶ If the ball gets stuck, quickly lower your foot and flick it over your opponent's leg (3).
- ▶ A good time to make a challenge is when your opponent is off-balance or has lost control of the ball.

Slide tackle

The slide tackle is a skilful and spectacular tackle. It is used when you are too far away from the attacker to jockey or make a block tackle. You end up on the floor so it is unlikely you will gain possession. For this reason the slide tackle is often used to make a clearance. The timing needs to be just right. You must make contact with the ball before the player or it is a foul.

- Approach from the side and keep your eyes on the ball (1).
- Lunge with the foot furthest from your opponent.
- Bend your supporting leg at the knee as you slide.
- Push or hook the ball to safety with your **instep** (2).
- It may be possible to trap the ball as you slide, get up quickly and move away with the ball.

Interceptions

Tackling is not the only way to win the ball. Cutting out an opponent's pass, or **intercepting**, is an excellent way of regaining possession. It leaves you with time and space to launch a quick **counter-attack**. Always be on the look-out to step in and steal the ball.
The trick is to judge the speed and flight of the opponent's pass.
Be patient; if you attempt an interception and fail, you are left out of position.

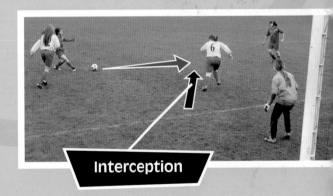

Interception

EXPERT: Gerard Piqué

Like many great defenders, Spanish star Gerard Piqué is great at reading the game. This means he can often tell where the ball is going to go next. He is always one step ahead of the attackers. When Piqué makes an interception he doesn't just hoof it upfield in hope. He can build attacks from defence with his accurate long passing.

CLEARING the ball

Above all else a defender should defend and stop attacks. If the defender is under pressure from an attacker there is no time for neat passing football. They should clear the ball away as far as possible.

Instep

1

Get rid of it

The key to a good clearance is plenty of height and distance. This takes the ball well away from the danger zone. If you can aim your clearance in the direction of a teammate, even better.

▶ A lofted drive is a good way of sending the ball high and long. Lean back and kick the lower area of the ball powerfully with your instep (1).

▶ You may have to **volley** your clearance if the ball is in the air. It is important to watch the ball closely as you kick it, and make a good contact (2).

2

Safety first

As a defender you can't take risks. Never try dribbling inside your own penalty area. Losing it to an attacker here could be a disaster. Do not pass across the face of goal either. If the pass is intercepted the striker will be through on goal. If it is not possible to clear the ball upfield, knock it off the side of the pitch instead. This is safe and gives time for your team to reorganise their defence.

Defensive headers

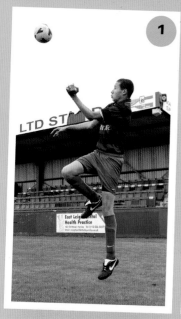

A clearing header also needs to be sent high and far. Defenders put the strength of their whole body behind the header to drive it away from goal.

▶ Push off firmly with one leg (1) and arch your back in the air.
▶ Keep your eyes open and aim to hit the bottom half of the ball with the middle of your forehead.
▶ Really attack the ball and strike it with your forehead moving upwards (2).

PRACTICE DRILL

Practise your defensive headers with a friend. Take it in turns to throw the ball to each other and see who can head it the furthest.

EXPERT:
Nemanja Vidic

The heading skills of Nemanja Vidic make him one of the best in the business. The defensive header is so important because it is often the last barrier between the attacker and the goal. Vidic wins his headers more often than not because he is brave and attacks the ball fiercely in a crowded penalty box. He also has great spring in his jump, which helps him tower above attackers (right).

POSITIONING

A defender must concentrate at all times, even if they are not challenging for the ball. They must constantly be moving their position on the pitch in relation to attackers and their fellow defenders. Positioning is a key part of defending.

Staying goal-side

Rule number one for a defender is to stay **goal-side** of their attacker. This means never letting the player you are marking between you and the goal (1). If you make this mistake, and the ball travels past you, your chance of challenging the attacker has probably gone (2).

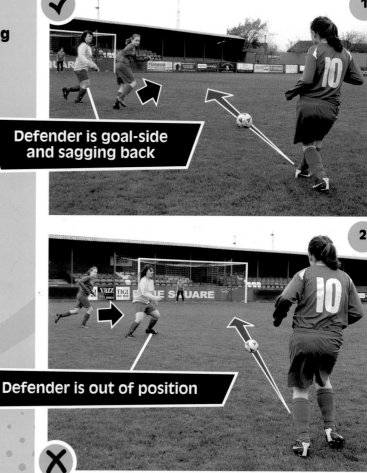

Defender is goal-side and sagging back

Defender is out of position

Closing down space

Always look to cover or mark attackers who are free and in space. Do this and your opponents will have nowhere to pass the ball. Don't get too close to the player you are marking, especially if they are quick. A quick burst of speed and they will be away from you. Hang back slightly from the attacker, to give you time to react to their run (1). This is called 'sagging back'.

Playing in formation

A team's defence must work together to stop the opposition's attacks. Most sides play a formation that has a line of four defenders at the back (right). The back four has two centre backs and two full backs. The back four must play as a tight unit. They should not be positioned too far away from each other when defending. All paths to goal need to be covered. If the defence leaves a huge gap the attackers will break through.

Centre backs – The main defenders, who play in front of the goalkeeper.

Full backs – They must have good defensive skills, but also be able to run down the wings to join attacks.

On the cover

Always look to support your teammates in defence. Be ready to move over and challenge an attacker who gets past the on-ball defender. For example, full backs often come across and cover behind their centre backs (below). Communication between defenders is vital. Shout to each other and make sure you are all in the best position.

Offside

Offside trap

An attacker is **offside** if there are less than two opponents between themselves and the goal when the ball is played. A defence can take advantage of this rule with good teamwork. Just before an attacking pass is made, all defenders can step up the pitch at the same moment to catch the attacker offside (above).

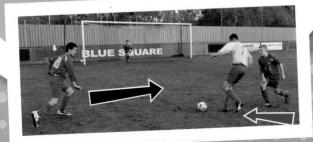

MARKING

A marking system is used by defensive line-ups so that everyone knows who should be covering which attacker.

There are two main ways in which a team marks players – man-marking and zonal marking.

Man-marking

Man-marking is where a defender marks a specific attacker, and sticks by them for the whole game. Attackers who are man-marked find it very hard to find space and have an effect on the match. Teams often choose to man-mark a particularly dangerous and skilful attacker. Man-marking is also useful because you can match up skills. For example, a quick defender can mark a pacy attacker.

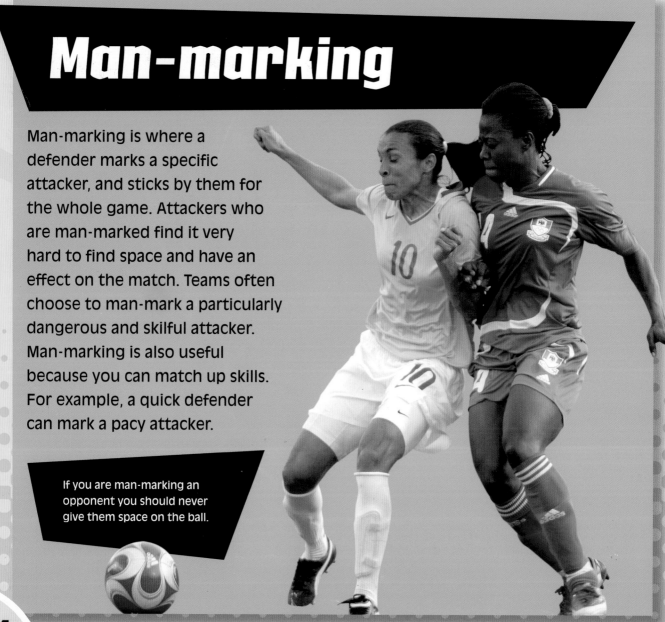

If you are man-marking an opponent you should never give them space on the ball.

Zonal marking

In a zonal-marking system each defender marks an area of the pitch (see below) instead of an individual player. Defenders mark attackers who enter their part of the pitch. A zonal system stops defenders being dragged out of position by their marker and leaving a hole in the defence. The defence can keep its shape and cover all areas of the pitch. The disadvantage is that the attackers are given more space. Again, communication between defenders is vital. Let a defender know if an attacker is entering their zone. A defence usually uses a mixture of zonal and man-marking in a game.

EXPERT: Casey Stoney

England's Casey Stoney (above, left) is not only a top defender, but also a great leader. She shouts at her defence, making sure they are marking the correct players, and are in the correct position. Stoney herself is an excellent man-marker. Her determination, strong tackle and ability to read the game keep even the best attackers in the world quiet. Stoney is also good at heading, so she often man-marks the opposing side's most dangerous aerial attacker.

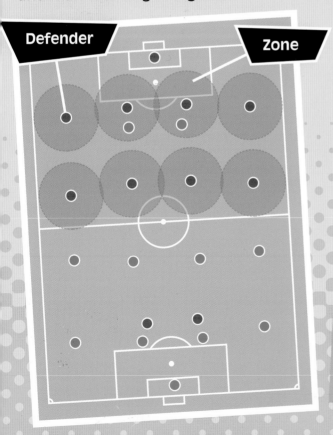

Defender

Zone

DEFENDING set pieces

Defending set pieces are key times in the match for a defence. There is a real danger of conceding a goal in these situations. Teams must organise their defence as soon as a free kick or corner is given. Defenders must concentrate and be alert.

Defending free kicks

A direct free kick in front of goal gives the attacking side a chance to shoot. You should build a defensive wall to block the shot.

▸ Put your tallest forwards and midfielders in the wall, leaving your defenders to mark other attackers.

▸ Line up the wall so that it covers one side of the goal. The goalkeeper covers the other side.

▸ Stand very close to each other, shoulder to shoulder, leaving no gaps.

▸ When the free kick is struck don't turn your back. Keep the wall firm and compact (left). You can protect yourself with your hands.

Free kicks from a narrower angle need defending with less players in the wall (right). The attacker is likely to cross the free kick into the box for a teammate. The defence usually organises a defensive line away from the goal. Any attackers hanging too close to the goal will then be offside. Defenders must mark opponents and fight to win the ball as the cross comes in.

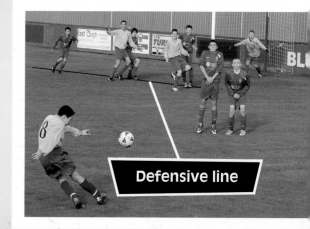

Defensive line

Indirect free kicks

Indirect free kicks must be touched by two players before a goal can be scored. The free-kick taker may try to tap the ball sideways for a teammate to shoot (right). Defenders must be ready to charge out to block any shot as soon as the free kick is taken.

Man-marker

Zonal marker

Defending corners

At a corner the defence must organise themselves, and know what each defender's job is. Players usually stand on the near and far post in a position to clear a shot off the line. Teams normally use a mixture of zonal and man-marking at corners. For example, one player must cover the zone in front of the near post, to stop any low corners reaching the middle of the penalty area (above). Other defenders will man-mark. They have to keep an eye on attackers running in from the edge of the box. Another defender should try to mark a player who is looking to receive a **short corner**.

Winning the second ball

Very often a set piece will be half-cleared away or flicked on by an attacker. Defenders must react quickly to the **second ball** and reach it before the attacker. They must also be alert to rebounds off the goalkeeper. Make sure you are first to the ball!

The GOALKEEPER

Goalkeepers have a huge responsibility. It is down to them to keep the ball out of the net. They have the chance to make a great save and be a hero. But there is no hiding place – a silly error will lead to a goal and possibly your team losing the match.

Goalkeeping stance

Keepers must always be ready for a shot on goal. The best position to be in is the **goalkeeping stance**.

▸ Keep your knees slightly bent and legs shoulder-width apart. Lean your body slightly forwards with your hands at the ready.

▸ To be ready to move quickly, you should always be on the balls of your feet. **Footwork** is key to good goalkeeping.

Catching

The best type of save to make is to catch the ball. The ball is then safely under control and the attack has ended.

Ground shots

▸ For a ground shot, try to move your body in line with the shot.

▸ Get down on one knee, with your body and legs behind the ball (1).

▸ Spread both hands next to each other, with your fingers pointing down. This forms a web to catch the ball.

▸ Catch the ball in a relaxed way, so the ball doesn't bounce out of your hands, and bring the ball safely towards your chest (2 and 3).

Overhead shots

- At this height, only your hands are between the ball and the goal, so watch the ball carefully.
- Catch with your hands spread behind the ball, this time with your fingers pointing up. Your thumbs should be touching (1).
- Catch the ball as early as possible, again with your hands relaxed. Remember: soft hands equal safe hands.
- You can try getting your body behind an overhead shot, by jumping up before quickly getting your hands behind the ball (2).

Waist-high shots

- As with a ground shot, get your body behind the ball and point your hands towards the ground.
- On impact, arch your body back to take the sting out of the shot, and cradle the ball safely (below).

Diving saves

From the goalkeeping stance, you are also ready to spring off and make a diving save. It is still possible to catch the ball as you dive.

- Take a step to the side and launch yourself into the air off one foot. Dive sideways, but slightly towards the ball.
- Catch with your bottom hand behind the ball and the other on top (above).
- Land on your side, not your stomach. As you land, gather the ball into your chest to prevent it from spilling out.

Deflecting SAVES

A powerfully struck shot or a dive at full stretch may mean a catch is impossible. The next best thing a goalkeeper can do is to deflect the ball away from goal.

Try not to deflect shots back out in front of goal to an attacker. Tipping the ball round the post or over the crossbar is a much safer save to make.

Round the post

To deflect a shot, your hands should get behind the flight of the ball. Then use your palms or fingertips to push the ball round the post. A double-handed save is stronger. But, at other times you have no option but to stretch and make the one-handed save. A one-handed save needs a very strong arm and wrist. Keep your arm tense and firm as you make the save.

Tipping it over

The tip-over is a good way of dealing with a powerful, high shot or a **lob** shot that is sailing over your head. Spring upwards off one foot (1) and reach up to push the ball with your palm or fingertips over the bar (2). For a lob shot you may have to **backpedal** before reaching up to make the save.

EXPERT:
Iker Casillas

Spanish goalkeeper Iker Casillas (right) has quickly become one of the best goalkeepers in the history of the game. In 2012 Casillas became the first player ever to win 100 matches for his country. His **agility** and quick reactions make him capable of pulling off the most extraordinary and breathtaking saves.

PRACTICE DRILL:
Double save

You cannot always deflect the ball from danger. A save from close-range or a shot that hits the post often gives the attacker a chance of a rebound. Keepers must have the agility to quickly spring up after making a save to stop the rebound. Practise this skill with a friend:

▸ Your friend shoots the ball to one side of the goal (1).
▸ Make the save, push the ball back out to them and get up quickly.
▸ Now scamper across goal and make another save as your friend shoots the rebound to the other side of the goal (2).
▸ Repeat this exercise for five minutes. It is great for a goalkeeper's fitness.
▸ Ask your friend not to shoot too hard, as it is just a training routine.

CROSSES

A goalkeeper should command their penalty area. They can see the game in front of them better than their teammates and they can give their defenders advice. The easiest way for a defence to deal with a ball into the box is for the keeper to come and claim it. The goalkeeper should shout their name clearly to let the defenders know that they are coming for the ball.

Claiming a cross

When a high ball comes into the penalty area goalkeepers have an advantage over other players. They can reach much higher with their hands than an attacker can with their head. This is how you do it.

▶ Spring up off one foot to help you gain height.
▶ As on overhead shots, get your hands behind the ball with your fingers spread like a web.
▶ Catch the ball as early as possible.
▶ Don't let the ball drop. Try to catch it at its highest point.

Defenders are always pleased to see their goalkeeper claim a cross and put an end to an attack.

Decision making

The secret to good goalkeeping is to make the right decisions. You must be able to judge when you can or cannot claim a cross. Getting it wrong is a common and costly mistake. If the goalkeeper comes out and does not reach the ball, the attacker may have the chance to score an **open-goal**. If you decide to go for the ball, call loudly, and be positive and determined.

Punching

Dropping a cross can also spell trouble. If you are coming for a cross through a crowd of players, a punch away may be safer. You need to get good distance on the punch.

▸ Clench your fists tightly together as you jump.
▸ With wrists firm, aim to punch just below the middle of the ball.
▸ On impact, straighten your arms, and jab the ball with a sharp stabbing action.

A goalkeeper punches the ball to safety. With so many players in his way a catch would be difficult and risky.

ONE-ON-ONES

In a one-on-one situation it is goalkeeper versus attacker. There are no defenders on hand to help. It is up to the goalkeeper to use all of their skills to outwit the attacker.

Positioning

A goalkeeper's positioning is crucial. They need to be in a place that gives them the best chance of saving the ball. Positioning is especially important in one-on-ones. You need to cover as many angles to goal as you can. You can narrow the angle by coming off your line and advancing towards the attacker (1). By moving forward, less of the goal is visible to the attacker. But, don't come off your line too soon or too far, as the striker could chip the ball over your head. If the attacker is approaching from the side, position yourself closer to the near post (2). You are then covering the side of the goal that is nearest the attacker. Goalkeeper's should never be beaten at their near post.

1

2

Make yourself big

While moving towards the attacker try to stay in the goalkeeping-stance position, so you are ready to make any kind of save. Keep your body upright and your arms outstretched to block as much of the goal as possible (1). If you fall to the ground before the attacker shoots, you have made their job easy. They can kick the ball over your body and into the net.

Reflexes

Shots from close range require excellent **reflexes**. Reflexes are quick reactions to a moving ball. Good goalkeepers make reflex saves with all parts of their body. They do whatever it takes to keep the ball out of the net. You can block a shot with your legs, chest and even your head.

Timing your dive

The timing of your dive is very important, whether it be to save a shot, or to smother the ball at the feet of an attacker dribbling around you. If you dive at the feet of an attacker too late and trip the player, you will give away a penalty and may be sent off.

Reflex save

EXPERT: Gianluigi Buffon

Gianluigi Buffon is the top goalkeeper from Italy and one of the best in the world. His nickname is Superman. A striker's shot has to be absolutely perfect to beat him. Buffon is nearly two metres tall and covers almost all of the goal with his huge frame and long-reaching arms.

DISTRIBUTION

A goalkeeper's job is not only to save. Once they have the ball they must also start their own team's attack. Distribution is an important skill and should not be underestimated. You can kick or throw the ball. A quick restart can catch the opposition out and start a fast counter-attack.

Throws

Throws tend to be more accurate than kicks but they cover less distance.

The roll – used for short distances
▶ Bend down slightly and distribute the ball using an underarm throw (1).
▶ Roll the ball to a player in space.
▶ It is usually safer to roll the ball out wide, to the opposite side from where the attack has just come.

Shoulder throw – for a quick, short throw
▶ Hold the ball in one hand and thrust forward using a bent arm (2).

Overarm throw – for longer distances
▶ Keep your feet on the ground with one foot in front of the other.
▶ Your front foot should point in the direction of the throw.
▶ Bring your arm back straight and swing it over in an arc (3 and 4).

Kicks

If distance is needed then a kick is usually the best option.

Volley

- ▶ Hold the ball in both hands.
- ▶ Take a short run-up at a slight angle to the direction of the kick.
- ▶ Plant your standing foot towards the target.
- ▶ Drop the ball from waist-high. Don't toss it upwards.
- ▶ Kick with your instep and follow through in line with the target.

Half volley

An alternative to the volley is to kick the ball just after it bounces (2 and 3). For this kick drop the ball from waist-high, but slightly in front of your body (1).

Goal kicks

A goal kick is awarded when the opponents knock the ball over the **goal line** to the side of the goal. Here the goalkeeper has to get power and height from off the ground.

- ▶ Approach at a slight angle and place your standing foot to the side of the ball (right).
- ▶ Get your foot under the ball with toes pointed outwards and strike with the inside of your instep. To stop the ball curling, hit it just on the inside of its centre.

Back passes

A pass back from a teammate cannot be picked up. If you have time, bring it under control and strike it like a goal kick. If you are under pressure you will have to hit it first time (right). Keep your eyes closely on the ball and make sure you clear it somewhere safe. Don't miss it!

27

DEFENSIVE stars

Here is a selection of some of the finest defenders and goalkeepers in the world today. These players are masters at keeping attackers at bay.

Each profile looks at the trophies the player has won individually and as part of a team.

Gianluigi Buffon

D.O.B: 28.01.78
Nation: Italy
Height: 1.91 m
Weight: 83 kg
International Caps 134

Club Record:

		Appearances
1995-2001	Parma	225
2001-	Juventus	437

Honours: UEFA Cup 1999; Italian Cup 1999; Italian League 2002, 2003, 2012, 2013; FIFA World Cup 2006

Top Award:
European Goalkeeper of the Year 2003

Vincent Kompany

D.O.B: 10.04.86
Nation: Belgium
Height: 1.90 m
Weight: 85 kg
International Caps/Goals 55 (4)

Club Record:

	Appearances	(Goals)
2003-2006 Anderlecht	102	(6)
2006-2008 SV Hamburg	49	(3)
2008- Manchester City	200	(7)

Honours: Belgian League 2004, 2006; FA Cup 2011; Premier League 2012

Top Award: Premier League Player of the Season 2012

Sergio Ramos

D.O.B: 30.03.86
Nation: Spain
Height: 1.83 m
Weight: 81 kg
International Caps/Goals 109 (9)

Club Record:

	Appearances	(Goals)
2003-2005 Sevilla	49	(3)
2005- Real Madrid	355	(41)

Honours: Spanish League 2007, 2008, 2012; European Championship 2008, 2012; FIFA World Cup 2010; Spanish Cup 2011

Top Award:
Spanish League Best Defender 2012

Nemanja Vidic

D.O.B: 21.10.81
Nation: Serbia
Height: 1.88 m
Weight: 84 kg
International Caps/Goals 56 (2)

Club Record:

	Appearances	(Goals)
2001-2004 Red Star Belgrade	95	(16)
2004-2005 Spartak Moscow	41	(4)
2005- Manchester United	268	(18)

Honours: Serbian League 2004; Premier League 2007, 2008, 2009, 2011, 2013; Champions League 2008; FIFA Club World Cup 2008

Top Award:
Premier League Player of the Season 2011

Gerard Piqué

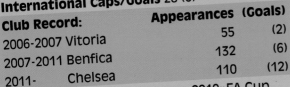

D.O.B: 02.02.87   **Nation:** Spain
Height: 1.92 m   **Weight:** 77 kg
International Caps/Goals 57 (4)

Club Record:	Appearances	(Goals)
2004-2008 Manchester United	23	(2)
2008- Barcelona	232	(16)

Honours: Premier League 2008; Champions League 2008, 2009, 2011; Spanish League 2009, 2010, 2011, 2013; Spanish Cup 2009, 2012; FIFA Club World Cup 2009, 2011; FIFA World Cup 2010;

Top Award:
UEFA Team of the Year 2012

David Luiz

D.O.B: 22.04.87
Nation: Brazil
Height: 1.89 m
Weight: 84 kg
International Caps/Goals 28 (0)

Club Record:	Appearances	(Goals)
2006-2007 Vitoria	55	(2)
2007-2011 Benfica	132	(6)
2011- Chelsea	110	(12)

Honours: Portuguese League 2010; FA Cup 2012; Champions League 2012; UEFA Europa League 2013

Top Award:
Portuguese League Player of the Year 2010

Hope Solo

D.O.B: 30.7.81
Nation: USA
Height: 1.75 m
Weight: 70 kg
International Caps 137

Club Record:	Appearances
2003 Philadelphia Charge	8
2004 Gothenburg FC	19
2005 Lyon	7
2009-2010 Saint Louis Athletica	23
2010 Atlanta Beat	16
2011 MagicJack	4
2012 Seattle Sounders	3
2013- Seattle Reign	14

Honours: Olympic Gold 2008, 2012; CONCACAF Gold Cup 2006;

Top Award: US Soccer Female Athlete of the Year 2009
US Goalkeeper of the Year 2009

Iker Casillas

D.O.B: 20.5.81
Nation: Spain
Height: 1.82 m
Weight: 70 kg
International Caps 149

Club Record:	Appearances
1999- Real Madrid	654

Honours: Spanish League 2001, 2003, 2007, 2008, 2012; UEFA Champions League 2000, 2002; European Championship 2008, 2012; FIFA World Cup 2010; Spanish Cup 2011; European Championship 2012

Top Award:
FIFA World Cup Golden Glove 2010

Statistics in this book are correct at the time of going to press, but in the fast-moving world of football are subject to change.

Glossary

agility the skill of moving quickly and easily

attributes the characteristics and skills a player has

backpedal move backwards quickly

closing down quickly surrounding opponents on the ball so they do not have space

counter-attack to turn defence into an attack

distribution the goalkeeper's release of the ball to their teammates

footwork the way in which you move your feet

goalkeeping stance the position a goalkeeper's body should be in as they get themselves ready for a shot on their goal

goal lines the lines at each end of a football pitch

goal-side a defensive position on the pitch where you are between your goal and your opponent

instep the area of the foot around the bootlaces

intercept to stop an opponent's pass reaching its destination

jockeying stopping an opponent on the ball moving forward, by staying on your feet and blocking their movement

lob to loft the ball over an opponent's head

man-marking a marking system where defenders guard a particular opponent

offside a position on the field where the ball cannot be passed to you. To be onside you must have two opponents between you and the opponents' goal.

one-on-one a chance for the striker to score, where they have just the goalkeeper to beat

open-goal an opportunity to score in a goal that is unguarded by a goalkeeper or defenders

positioning the skill of being in the correct position on the pitch at the right time

possession if a teammate or yourself has control of the ball then your team is in possession

reflexes quick reactions to a moving ball

second ball a term which describes the ball when it has gone loose after touching another player, such as a rebound off the goalkeeper

set piece a move carried out by a team as they return the ball into play, such as a corner or free kick

short corner a corner which is passed short to a teammate instead of crossed into the penalty area

volley to strike the ball before it has touched the ground

zonal marking a marking system where defenders are given a particular zone on the pitch to cover

Further information

Books

Football Skills, Clive Gifford, Kingfisher, 2005

Goalkeeper (Talking About Football), Clive Gifford and Antony Lishak, Franklin Watts, 2006

Master the Game: Defender, Paul Broadhurst and Andy Allen, Hodder Arnold, 2008

Soccer: Defending (Know the Game), A & C Black, 2007

John Terry and Rio Ferdinand (Football All-Stars), Rory Callan, 2013

Football (Go Turbo), Tom Palmer, Franklin Watts, 2009

Websites

www.footy4kids.co.uk/defending_tackling_drills.htm
This site has tips and practice drills to help you improve your defending and tackling.

www.videojug.com/tag/football-defensive-moves
See video footage of the key defensive skills needed.

http://keeper-skool.com/category/education
A website dedicated to goalkeeping.

http://soccerlens.com/football-legends-defender/21859/
A look back at the best defenders to ever play the game.

Note to parents and teachers: Every effort has been made by the Publishers to ensure that these websites are suitable for children, that they are of the highest educational value, and that they contain no inappropriate or offensive material. However, because of the nature of the Internet, it is impossible to guarantee that the contents of these sites will not be altered. We strongly advise that Internet access is supervised by a responsible adult.

DVDs

Winning Soccer Vol 7 - Goalkeeper Training, Quantum Leap, 2008

Soccer Tactics: Defending to Win, Quantum Leap, 2006

Index